I AM

THE

SOULUTION

8 Transformational Approaches To Turning

Obstacles Into Opportunities

Curtis D. Jasper, PhD

7 Publishing

www.7-publishing.com

Los Angeles, California

ISBN-13: 978-0692651179
ISBN-10: 0692651179

Editor Jennifer Wilkes

Copyright © Dr. Curtis Jasper

All rights reserved. No part of this book may be reproduced in any form or by any electronic or mechanical means, including information storage and retrieval systems, without written permission from the publisher or author, except in the case of a reviewer, who may quote brief passages embodied in critical articles or in a review.

Book Cover Design by Saba Tekle

DEDICATION

To my incredible wife, Angela, who has always supported me long before you gave me your hand and heart in marriage. You continued to love me when I struggled loving myself. I AM forever grateful for you.

To my children AA, JR, JJ & JJ, may you all create lives that you love and continue to be the blessings that you are. Thank you, very much, for choosing me as your life partner.

To my mother, no words would ever describe my love for you. Thank you for being my guardian angel and spiritual warrior. Thank you for loving me unconditionally and allowing me to always be TRUE to who I thought I should be. May you continue to Rest well.

To the memory of my father, who will always remain in my heart as someone who continuously tried to connect, communicate and create with me when I was completely against it. The roots you provided me and the belief you held for me has completely shaped the person I AM today. Thank you, dad. Thank you, All!

DR. CURTIS JASPER

CONTENTS

Acknowledgments

1	Longing for a Greater Expression of Life	1
2	True Life Cannot Be Contained By Labels	13
3	When Was the Last Time I Did Something for the First Time?	26
4	Courage: Tell the Story of Who You Are with Your Whole Heart	37
5	I Decided to Be Childlike	52
6	More to Me Than I Have Given a Chance To	64
7	My Answers to Life's Answers	76
8	Transformational Approaches	81
	Open Letter to My Father	89
	About the Author	94

ACKNOWLEDGMENTS

I AM deeply grateful for my wife, my children and my parents for shaping me into the Being I AM now. I AM also deeply grateful for all the individuals whom I attracted for my own personal, professional and private growth regardless of the outcomes, the lessons learned were invaluable.

- Chapter 1 -
Longing for a Greater Expression of Life

It dawned on me one day, *Why do I feel like I'm not really doing what I was called to do?* I mean life had its joyful moments, but it didn't possess the pizzazz I once had. I was getting tired of waiting for that feeling of being in my zone - the feeling of exhilaration, of power, of joy, of energy. I lost my way of self-expression. I needed a platform to share my thoughts, my feelings, my outlooks on life, and my world…the world.

For the last three or more years, I've been longing to get back to the place where I served the people – any group of people – in some capacity, but I've been in a protective state of comfort. I've been shut out from the world, and into my made-up world of protection.

I was hurting from losses. I was hurting from gains. Hell, I was hurting from being hurt. I struggled to remind myself of the awesome feeling of sharing who I was with the rest of the world. I gave up the limits of self-expression in the former chosen field of education, due to limits and conformity.

I know my voice is my tool to use to create along with my mind. I have now regained my conscious awareness of utilizing the one mind - the universal intelligence we all possess.

*Note to self:

Self-healing must come first. If we think we can guide our brother aright while our own feet still walk in darkness, we are mistaken. We must first clarify our own vision. Then we shall become as lights illuminating the way for others. But, can we teach a lesson we have not yet learned? Can we give that which we do not possess? To suppose so is hypocrisy - a thing to be shunned. Jesus tears the mantle unreality from the shoulders of hypocrisy winnowing from the soul of sham and shallowness, its last shred of illusion. We cannot see reality until our eyes are open and until the light of eternal truth has struck deeply into our own souls.

i.

Standing in the Midst of a Discordant Fact Knowing Something is Better For Me

Death, divorce, depression, and depletion were clearly occupying my mind and my entire thought process. I didn't realize that, although I wasn't sure I was completely depressed, I was in a protective cocoon state so that I could make some sense of my world. I lost my mother to lung cancer, my father to a number of ailments, my wife and family to divorce, my business ventures and income to depression and neglect, and my energy and excitement for living to depletion. I knew all of this was happening for my greater good, but I couldn't shake the feeling of spiritual exhaustion.

I spent the last monies from my business ventures to focus only on having a great time (outside of spending time with my children) a few meager business affairs, and working out at the gym. I guess I wasn't clinically classified for depression because I wasn't diagnosed by a medical professional. I didn't receive meds, nor did I completely neglect my daily responsibilities and relinquish any of my close relationships with friends and family.

Because I never completely lost my desire to inspire people, I chose to pursue it only on a small level or casually. I didn't see a need to play it out fully during this time. But in the midst of my checking out, I stood as best I could in knowing that something better was for me. I just wasn't ready to take it on.

Note to self:

Know your own mind. Train yourself to think what you wish to think. Be what you wish to be. Feel what you wish to feel. And place no limit on principle. The words which you speak will be just as powerful as the words which Jesus spoke. You must note within, and not merely accept it with your intellect, that your word is the law where unto it is sent. If you reach a point where your inner consciousness believes, then your word is simply an announcement of reality. Know without a shadow of doubt that as a result of your treatment, some action takes place in the infinite mind. The infinite mind is the actor, and you are the announcer. If you have a vague, subtle, and unconscious fear be quiet and ask yourself, "Who am I? What am I? Who is speaking? What is my life?" In this matter, think right back to principle until your thought becomes perfectly clear again - such is the power of right thinking that it cancels and erases everything unlike itself.

ii.

Life Is Trying to Come at Me From Infinite Directions

Because I had chosen to become a seeker of awareness quite some time ago, life appeared to come to me from a number of directions personally and professionally. Most of the challenges I either ignored or simply didn't give serious thought to. Instead of being a doer, as I had always been, I chose to become a spectator. I chose to stand on the sideline and critique my own life. I chose to focus on the how and remain in the intellectual mode of thinking as opposed to having a spiritual mindset. I chose to use force instead of power. I knew using force would be my way of trying to make something happen out of nothing while simultaneously focusing on what was missing from my life. My life continued in the direction of my focused energy. I felt my thoughts were conflicted, which caused me to struggle really hard to remain centered.

I hated my life at the time. I didn't hate it enough to end it or anything like that, but I was completely disappointed because what I was currently experiencing wasn't what I had planned for myself. For the last decade my plan was to raise a family, be happily married, contribute to my extended family and community, change the world, and make a ton of money doing it. I wanted to live life on my own terms – working for myself, but not by myself.

The more I tried to use force, the more things would work out for a while then eventually require more force to sustain. My life was trying to come to me from an infinite number of directions, but none of them were good. None of them felt good. I knew there had to be another way. I opened my eyes then closed my eyes to meditation and continued until change began to surface.

Note to self:

God can only give us what we are willing to take.

God cannot give us anything unless we are in a mental condition to receive the gift. The law cannot do anything for us unless it does it through us. Belief is absolutely necessary to correct demonstration. You are on the path of experience just waking to the real fact of your true being. As we awake, we find we are surrounded by many false conditions. But there's something within which remembers the real state. If you will sit in quiet contemplation of good, as an inner experience, you will experience the good which you contemplate. One can do this only as he or she turns from that which is evil and dwells on the good alone. The universe will not be divided.

iii.

At Least I Loved

Divorce for men – at least for me – brings a ton of things I had no idea even existed. Even talking with divorcees and a therapist, no one or nothing could have prepared me for the emotional roller coaster my divorce took me on. At one point, I loved my ex-wife. I adored the ground she walked on. She was beautiful, smart, and a great mother. However, she always remained guarded which didn't allow us to grow together. After 11 years and a number of other challenges, we chose to end the marriage. I thought it was the best thing, and I still do. But I had no idea the emotions would be devastating.

Being out of control emotionally was something I had never experienced. Every moment, every second, every minute, every hour, and every day was a challenge. I hated waking up in the morning – or, in my case, in the afternoon. I faced the arduous task of trying to control what I thought about and my feelings to tackle my day. I hated waking up for months because I didn't want to know that I was at the mercy of my feelings, and there was nothing I could do to change it. So I decided to just be with my feelings instead of analyzing or judging them. I chose to just be with my feelings until they passed. If I was feeling angry, I stopped whatever I was doing and just sat still without saying a word to anyone until I started feeling better. I began to focus on just trying to feel better - not good, not great, just better than I had felt the moments prior.

One of the ways I chose to feel better about my divorce was to focus on being grateful for the experience of my marriage, the children from my marriage, the wife I had chosen, and the good times we had. I tried not to focus on the challenging times, but most times that was pretty difficult. As with everything, it became easier as time went on. When the bad thoughts surfaced, I forced a grin on my face to try to convince my brain that I was happy. After a while, I really started to feel good. I woke up and retired my day by reminding myself that my marriage was a precious gift from a Universal Intelligence and that I was grateful for the experience. I started telling myself repeatedly, *At least I loved*, which was the greatest feeling of all.

iv.

The Part of Me That Was Hurt Was Not the Real Me

I could recall countless events that happened in my life. But I'm only focusing on the last few years in this particular book: experiencing the disappointment of a failed marriage, the death of my mom, failed businesses, and even finding out that I had an adult daughter, all within the last three years from the beginning of 2009 until late 2011. What I learned was when I think back to the experiences that were the most painful, the part that was hurt was my ego. It was bruised. It was injured. I took things very personally. I was okay with the death of my mom because once she shared that she had lung cancer- after smoking for 40 years and walking through that journey of taking her back and forth to hospital visits, treatment, chemo, and radiation for over a year- I just gradually went into acceptance. I used that time to really connect and just be with her. When she finally transitioned in March 2010, I was okay. I wasn't great, but I was okay. However, it did impact me, but I didn't realize it at the time.

The ending of my marriage was very difficult. During my divorce proceedings, we were separated, so we were sharing the kids. We lived in close proximity. Meanwhile, I had gone to my 20th high school reunion and found out I had a grown daughter, an adult daughter whom I hadn't known about. Because she was conceived while I was in high school, she was 22 when I found out about her. I brought her into my life and introduced her to my wife at the time. And although we were still trying to hold on, we weren't deliberately working on the marriage.

During the decline of my marriage and the death of my mom, my business ventures plummeted. I wasn't doing any new business. I had been very successful in real estate at the time and accumulated a lot. I'd built several businesses, investments, and management businesses. I invested a lot of time and money in becoming trained to learn a system that provided me success. But then I checked out. I just went into a cocoon. I thought I was depressed. I started spending money only on having a good time. Although I had the money, I wasn't paying my bills. I just didn't feel like it. I watched my life crumble. I thought I was depressed or functionally depressed. But, I realize now that I just went into a cocoon, a protective area that could kind of soften the blows. I put on – I like to think that I put on one of those sparing hats that you see when boxers are sparing. I knew I was getting hit, but I put the protective head gear on and just took the blows without really swinging or putting up my guard. The hits that were most painful were to my ego and my spirit. I had to learn how to resurface my spiritual energy and connect with the one mind, the God source that I knew was in me that had pulled me through in other areas at other times. So, it wasn't the real me; it was my ego. And although the ego is a part of me, when it's managed properly it gets me through some times where I'm doubting myself. Overall, I learned that when my life had been the most painful, the part of me that was hurt was not the real me; it was my ego. It wasn't my oneness with the most high. This wasn't good or bad, just what was so.

*Inspired in part or whole by The Original Science of Mind Public domain Text by Ernest Holmes.

- Chapter 2 -
True Life Cannot Be Contained By Labels

I hated labels. I hated labels coming up as a child. I hated labels in high school as a teenager and as a young adult. And I'm not talking about labels that refer to when someone calls someone else a name. I'm talking about official labels that have been established by society, by the mass consciousness, by everybody, and by the world. I realized that my life could not be contained and would not be contained by labels.

I didn't like the word "boss". Those labels symbolized a sense of control, and I didn't want to be controlled. I wanted to express myself and find my own way. So I chose for myself, and I reminded myself through these last few years that my life would not contain labels and that I would not try to make sense out of it by way of labels. I would use my awareness. I wouldn't waste time labeling my life, my experiences and my happiness because I thought that labeling them would cause me to limit them, to table them and say thing's like, "Oh, things is great. This is good. I'm successful. I'm a failure. I hate that. I hate this." Once I labeled it, it didn't allow me an opportunity to go back and reexamine it. It only caused me to label it as a file and set it on my mental shelf. I realized that doing that kept me stuck and kept me in the past. When I labeled garbage file folders and it was time for me to withdraw from them, they weren't good. I figured if I didn't try to analyze and subsequently label them, then I could just make sense out of my world by just allowing and detaching. I wanted to have things happening without names. I wanted to have a nameless life for a minute. Even after completing my doctorate, I didn't necessarily want to use the word "doctor". I turned to using my initials because it reminded me of good days like when my college buddies first gave me the initials C.J. It just reminded me of a good time. So, I heavily relied on C.J. Outside of the business world, I began introducing myself socially as C.J. And, although using the initials was in fact a label, it still kept me in a feel-good space, so I didn't see it quite as a label. I stopped using Curt Jasper, Curtis Jasper, or even Curtis D. Jasper when I started introducing myself. I just thought that labels contained me and limited my self-expression. So, I decided that my life – true life – cannot be contained by labels.

When my divorce was finalized I chose not to tell people that I was divorced. Not that I was hiding, but again, I wanted to refrain from using labels. When or if anyone asked, I would simply say, "No. I'm not married." Or "I'm no longer married," as opposed to using the term 'divorced'. Again, standing in alignment with what felt good for me spiritually, at the time, this was another opportunity for me to not use a label by referring to my ended marriage as a divorce. I was clear that divorce was a legal term and an event, and I was no longer married. So, I just decided to use "I'm no longer married."

When I refer to my ex-spouse, I simply use her name. Again, it kept me in alignment with my true life. My new life would not contain labels. I wouldn't indicate whether I was single, divorced, or anything like that. I would just share where I was currently, depending on the subject. The life

I chose for myself – my true life - cannot be contained by labels.

In my opinion, labels keep one stuck in the past. It doesn't allow for future self-expression, or even current expression. Never limit your view of life to any past experience, which in my opinion, labels cause. The possibility of life is inherent within the capacity to imagine what life is, backed by the power to produce this imagery or divine imagination. It's not a question of failing, succeeding, or naming things with labels to keep them within a current perspective. It's simply a matter of sticking to an idea – a new idea – without a label until it becomes a tangible reality. It's the illusion in the way we look at things when they are contained by labels. So we must look at harmony, happiness, plentifulness, prosperity, peace, and correct action until they appear, but not limit them with labels for different areas of our life.

i.

If It Does Not Make You Come Alive, It Is Too Small for You

Anything or anyone that does not make you come alive is too small for you. When I use the word 'alive', I mean filled with energy or spirit or whichever one you choose to use. From age 39 to 40, I was gradually sorting out anything or anyone that didn't bring me alive. I met a ton of people during the last three years from all walks of life, personally and professionally. I met great friends from friends from friends. I met colleagues, business associates, contractors, sub-ordinates, everyone. But then I went into a spiritual purging, and I realized that anything or anyone that wasn't bringing me positive energy, a high level of energy – and I don't mean temporary energy, I mean energy from a spiritual and joyful place – it was too small. They were too small for me, I was using this as a spring-board to go to the next phase of my life. I used turning 40. I used death and I used birth as a new beginning, as a rebirth, not a death, but a rebirth. I used all the literal deaths that had happened, as a rebirth for me. Part of me moving to the next phase of my life at 40 was that I was going to eliminate things and people that did not do it for me. When I saw, them, and if I didn't immediately become alive, I wanted to eliminate them. That even went for things in the media, that went for people, friends and family, different objects, and different sources of entertainment. I eliminated certain foods and snacks –

anything that didn't do it for me.

I also added things. I increased my workout, which obviously improved my health and wellness. I started working on my spiritual journey, reading tons and tons of books, and joined a church for a while. I started going to the church's classes, keeping in touch with my loved ones, and reaching out to my friends on a daily basis through social network. I figured I wasn't going to die immediately for things that weren't keeping me alive but I wasn't going to allow the things that weren't inspiring me to hang around, at least in the manner in which they once did. I wanted to use them as lessons. I wanted to be present. I wanted to thank the creative intelligence for allowing me to gain clarity on my journey. But I didn't want to consciously choose to hang out with certain people, talk to certain people, or engage in certain things that didn't make me happy while on my journey joyful.

Not from an external standpoint, but as I was in this state of being, I paid attention to how I felt and how it felt to me from a spiritual standpoint – not just through my senses. For example, if I chose to go out to a particular restaurant with a particular friend or group of friends, at some point I would become silent and take it all in through all of my senses and take a moment to choose for myself, *Is this good for me?* And if it was, I'd continue. But if it wasn't, I didn't necessarily discontinue it, but I would remind myself to look at other options. I figured, if I wanted to be impactful one day, or if I was working on being successful, that I had to eliminate any-thing or anyone that did not bring me alive. What was fortunate was that once I started to focus on this from an awareness standpoint, things started coming and going with very little effort from me. A lot of removal were painful because I didn't necessarily see them coming. But once I decided to detach and just allow things to transition, they were all good. Some things were too small, and I knew they were too small. But, I didn't want them all to leave. I was in denial.

Some things were huge, and they left – or at least I thought they were huge, but they were in fact small in terms of what they were providing for me. So again, once I became aware and once I chose to focus on my truth that anything or anyone that didn't bring me alive was too small for where I said I was going and that I was to live my life to the fullest, I started eliminating them.

ii.

100 Percent Responsible

Part of choosing to be 100 percent responsible for the experience of my experiences is that I had to step outside of my body (spiritually speaking) and really not place blame on anyone or anything. I focused on being grateful. That was a responsibility because things were not happening as well as I thought. I chose to be grateful for all those by taking 100 percent responsibility and acknowledging the Most High for being grateful. When things happened to me that weren't so good, I chose to be grateful for the experience, for the journey, and for going through it. Having those experiences provided me with clarity on things that I wanted; versus the things that I didn't want. It lifted a burden when I chose to be 100 percent responsible for the experience of my experiences, because it allowed me to not place blame on anyone or anything – not even on myself. If I made a mistake, I just chose not to do it. If I were in the midst of making a mistake, I chose to simply stop. I started journaling so that I could come back to focus on being responsible for the things I missed. If it was a painful experience, I journaled so that I could be 100 percent responsible.

Again, I chose to be grateful and acknowledged the things that happened. I chose to be grateful for the things that happened that wasn't going very well. I chose to not place blame, and I chose to celebrate myself. And that was another responsibility. I wanted to celebrate the good things. I wanted to acknowledge the not so good things. But I wanted to wake up– and remain awakened, I don't mean literally, I mean spiritually become awake to all of my happenings. And that awareness caused me to be 100 percent responsible for the experience. It was that responsibility, that high level of responsibility, which allowed me to grow. I also chose to be 100 percent responsible for the experience of my experience by detaching from the outcome. Once I declared something within, using the words 'I am,' or 'I am feeling great,' 'I am grateful,' or whatever I chose after the words 'I am,' that was my way of being responsible. If I was sad, I would say, "I am sad," and I would just be with that feeling until it passed on to a better feeling. For me, that was also taking 100 percent responsibility. And when I wanted to blame someone – about something I didn't agree with or friends, family, or significant other who said or did something I didn't appreciate – I would take responsibility for how I felt.

I, also, allowed people to have their own level of responsibility whether they chose to have it or not. I chose to take 100 percent responsibility for the experience of my experiences, only.

iii.

My World Expands and Contracts Based on How I Participate

The funny thing about life is that you've heard this saying, "If you're not growing, you're dying because there's no such thing as staying still in life." Everything moves through a season; the grass, the insects, the animals, and the seasons. So when I thought about this chapter, the title immediately reminded me of a choice; a choice to either wake up and create a world based on new thoughts, refreshed thoughts or let it contract based on old thoughts. Thinking is like working out at the gym. The more you use it, the bigger your world becomes.

One of the things I do is wake up choosing an original thought.

Most of this thinking is based on challenging myself to be spontaneous. If I'm spontaneous, I can always sustain my individuality, and part of that individuality is remaining spontaneous. Making plans and sticking to structure causes you to become something or someone else after a while. The predictability of that causes one to take the safe road – to fly under the radar. Therefore, when it's time to create new possibilities for myself, if I'm not purposely focusing on choosing new thoughts to create new outcomes, then it's 'not choosing' new thoughts (which is still a choice) which ultimately becomes responsible for contracting my life. Thus, my participation in my world is expanded or contracted based on how I'm participating from a thought process.

iv.

Willing and Becoming What I Am Capable Of

I'm made or unmade by myself. In the armory of my thoughts I forge weapons that either destroy or create myself or things that I'm involved in. Therefore, I create tools with which I can build myself; and those tools, obviously, are my thoughts. By right choice and true application of those thoughts, I can ascend to divine perfection. And by the abuse and wrong application of those thoughts, I can descend below dangerous levels. But between these areas – the two extremes – are all the grades of my character, and it's where I'm either made or not made to be the master of my life. Of all the beautiful truths pertaining to my soul, which have been restored and brought to light by my physical form, none are more fruitful of divine promise and confidence than the truth that I'm the master of my thoughts, the molder of my character, and the maker and shaper of my condition, environment, and destiny.

As being a power, intelligence, a love, and the creator of my own thoughts, I hold the key to every situation, and I contain within myself that transforming and regenerative agency by which I make for myself what I will. I am the master of my fate. Even in the weakest and abandoned state, it's important that I always gain control of my thoughts so that they can begin to reflect upon my condition.

My job was to pay attention to certain sign posts, to stay in the recognition stage, to remain optimistic. That's where I will watch my life become what I'm capable of manifesting. That's the universal law which isn't personal. It means whatever I focus on will focus on me. Whatever energy I send out will fully return back to me. I remember during the three year strain in my life from 2008 to 2011, I was willing to be comfortable. I was willing to be protected and it was a drastic decline in major areas to me, but it still felt good at the moment. I guess I was in a sense getting exactly what I was putting out in the universe. I still knew that I could have in my life whatever I was willing to be. I chose to be less ambitious and more reserved. Therefore, that's what I received.

- CHAPTER 3 -
When Was the Last Time I Did Something for the First Time?

"Man has an inherent power by which he may grow in whatsoever direction he pleases. And there does not appear to be any limit to the possibilities of his growth." -Wallace D. Wattles, author of *The Science of Success: The Secret to Getting What You Want*

I realized without doing something for the first time or coming up with an original thought to do something for the first time I wasn't growing. Most of us know that man is formed for growth, and he's under the necessity of growth. Life without progress becomes unendurable. The person who ceases to grow – who ceases from growth –

must either become dull or dead. There's no possibility in any of us that's not in all of us. But if we proceed with this level of comfort by not forcing ourselves to come up with an original thought or to do something for the first time, it stunts our growth. I realize there's a principle of power in all of us, and by the intelligent use and direction of this principle of power, we can develop our own mental faculties to come up with any and everything. So, if it's possible for us to think of it, it's obviously possible for it to take place in a physical form.

There are undreamed possibilities in common lives all around us, though there are no common people. Most of us believe we're common. It has always been, and always will be in the times of national or local stress, a rise of a lot of heroes or heroines through the quickening of the principle of power within. There's a genius in every man and woman waiting to be brought forth in every neighborhood, every city, every suburb, every town, every block, every subdivision, every school, and every job. There's a genius in every man and woman, and it's just waiting to come out. It has no vehicle to come out unless we do something for the first time or go forth with the thought we once had that we decided to bury within us.

Every area of the world has a great man or woman – someone to whom we all go to for advice in the time of need or trouble or someone who is instinctively recognized as being great in wisdom or insight. These people do small things in great ways. They are recognized as being great. They can do greater things. We all could, if we undertook those small ideas of doing things for the first time and really putting them into action. The principle of power gives us just what we ask for just how we ask for it if we only undertake the little things. It only gives us power for the little things. But if we try to do great things in a great way, it gives us all the power there is.

Note to Self:

The awakening of the principle of power in man is the real conversion - the passing from death to life. It is when the dead hear the voice and come forth and live. It is the resurrection and the life. When the power is awakened, man becomes the highest, and all power is given to him in heaven and on Earth. Nothing was ever in any man that is not in you and me. No man ever had more spiritual or mental power than you and I can attain or did greater things than you and I can accomplish or have yet to accomplish. We all can become what we want to be.

The last time I did something for the first time was beginning this book, this project, this thesis, this dissertation, a number of books, this transcript, and just getting my thoughts down on paper. This was the last time I did something for the first time. I've been contemplating this for years. I've had this on my goal list for the last 10 years or more actually. So, I chose today to do something every week for the first time, whether it's viewing a movie, reading something, or meeting someone.

I now stay in a discovery stage. I like to. When I wake up in the morning, one of the affirmations I use is "I wonder…" It's actually a question in the form of an affirmation "…what wonderful people I'll meet today? I wonder what new opportunities I'll be involved in today. What great things will happen to me today?"

Part of my reason for doing that is to remind myself to look for something new so that I can do it for the first time. Now, I don't always position myself to remember to do it on a daily basis, but rarely do I allow a week to go by where I haven't chosen to do something I haven't done for the first time. This is to sustain my individuality and spontaneity. It also brings me enjoyment and allows me to stay present knowing that if I'm working or trying something out for the first time, I've maintained a certain amount of presence – as opposed to when doing something I've always done or talking about something I plan on doing but hadn't started it yet...thinking of the past.

Therefore, I remind myself that causation is from within. I have to start from within by reminding myself that I showed up to do something great, in my life. I realize I create my own world by the way I think, and the more I want to create, the more I have to put out new thoughts to think new thoughts.

I chose to integrate my way of being and line it up with the universal laws because I know they are impersonal. There's a law that I use called the Law of Resistance, and it simply states that when you resist something, you magnify and give power to whatever you're resisting. This allows us to focus on something that isn't working, and, again, feeling like we must make something happen which allows us to focus more on what isn't working, and so more things come up.

There's also a lot that I learned from John

Maxwell's Law of Diminishing Intent, which he mentions in one of his books. I've read several of them, but this law indicates that the longer you take to put an idea or to put something into action, the less energy and excitement you have around it to sustain that action, once you get it going. Many times it's just good to try some new things sometimes on a smaller scale. I try a number of things without even mentioning them to anyone. And if they go over well, I smile; and if they don't go over well, I smile.

I chose to live my life by focusing on a weekly basis about 'when was the last time I did something for the first time?

i.

So Much of My Misery Lies in the Energy of Not Having

So much of my misery lies in the energy of not having. It seems like the more I focused on the things I didn't have, like money, the more I got what I focused on - which was not having money (more of The Law of Resistance!). Believe me; the universe takes you, your thoughts, and your words literally. There was a time in the business world when I chose for myself, I chose big, and then when I got up the next day and it was time to put those business practices in place, things seemed to kind of just show up. Once I made a choice and attacked it with energy and excitement as if I couldn't fail (even if I did), it would just be my way of showing myself that there must be an easier way. I sought out for that, but I also realized that when there were things that I desired that caused me grief, I knew it was the grief I was focusing on.

Many times I didn't realize that because I had put the emphasis on not having things. I had to remind myself and just choose whatever it was I wanted. If I wanted money, then I chose money. I stopped worrying about not having the money because when I focused on not having it, I was choosing more of not having it. For example, let's take my stack of bills. Every month when I ran out to my box to get my bills, I would grab the entire stack and place it in front of me on my desk. Part of the reason I still don't pay bills online is because I like the excitement, the energy, and the spiritual attachment of physically writing out the checks and blessing myself and the universe for allowing me to receive goods and services, most of them upfront. I get to receive the lights first with the promise of paying the light company later. One of the prayers I send out before I write out my bills is that I know that I have enough money, and then some, to pay all of my bills. I'd write them out first before I checked my bank balance knowing that it was always enough in my account to pay all of my bills. It was that energy of focusing on having, as opposed to not having, that created more of the having. I've spoken to colleagues, friends, and family and they say, "Oh, I hate paying bills. I don't even open my bills. I just get them and set them to the side because I know I don't have the money to pay them, or I have to wait until to payday." The friends who waited until payday associated payday with not having because the days they got paid were the days they wrote out their bills.

A day to reward yourself after you've paid your taxes and insurance, Uncle Sam, and other things could be a day of enjoyment, if you choose to look at it that way. Focusing on not having gives us more of that. Bless your bills, and bless any amount of money it takes to sustain your lifestyle instead of looking at your payday as bill paying time which is what sustains the misery surrounding the energy of not having. That's just one way that I chose to eliminate my misery as it

ii.

I Lost My Way

How did I lose my way? I simply fell asleep. At some point, we've all had times in our lives when things seemed effortless, whether we play the safe role and lined up everything where it was kind of fool proof with a few glitches, or we didn't take risk and kind of did the things we knew we could achieve with very little effort. But then there comes a time where you just kind of check out. Even if you're doing well. After a while, I started feeling like I was just losing my way. Although I may have been doing well by some people's standards, it was pretty bad to me. One day I just asked myself, *How did I lose my way? How did I get here after three years of sort of piddling around? The* best answer I could come up with was that I simply fell asleep.

I went to sleep on my life, and what I mean by that is I purposely stopped being conscious. I didn't want to employ the very laws, affirmations, prayers, and treatments that I knew had done me well. It's almost like I was punishing myself, and I chose to not use the tools – the ways of being that I knew had worked in the past – because I needed to be with my feelings. I needed to absorb the feelings around my mom's death, my divorce, some of the bad business decisions, and dealing with my children - all of my children.

I chose to lose my way. I didn't realize it until much later, but in essence I did choose it. I just went through the motions. I fell asleep. I decided to remain unconscious because I figured if I stopped with all the efforts of creating new things, then I wouldn't have to work so hard and be let down, if things didn't work out. A lot of times, as people, we fall asleep. Some of us remain asleep for a lifetime. As children, we always dreamed. We couldn't wait to tell anybody we ran into what we were going to be or what we were working on. But, we were always awake, no matter what. Then society, friends, family, and a mass consciousness stifled us. It caused us to be what they termed 'realistic.' It taught us to be predictable not individual, and to go along with the group.

After a long while of that treatment by teachers, community, and parents, we gradually fall asleep. Many times adults stifle our ability to be awake beginning from the time we are born. We learn at home that there are certain rules we must follow, certain structures, and certain parameters. After following directions as a child, most of us took those limitations right into adulthood. We look up years later, and ask ourselves, *How did I lose my way?*

I thought I had lost my way a few times especially during my marriage. I actually had lost my way by the end of the marriage, and that's because of a number of major incidents which came about. I didn't lose my way in the marriage, but I was doing the things I didn't want to do. I wasn't going in the way I wanted to go. I wasn't lost, yet. I was simply following a way that caused me to utilize too much effort. So, I chose to fall asleep, but there was a cost to that. The payoff was that I was able to get on the other side and share how I got to the other side with those behind me.

- Chapter 4 -
Courage: Tell the Story of Who You Are with Your Whole Heart

What does it mean to be courageous? Many times we are highly criticized for being courageous. One thing I found to be very useful in any and all of my relationships, both personal and professional, was to tell a story of who I was with my whole heart. I chose to do that after much thought and studied to do it without utilizing a big or drama-filled story. I chose to tell who I was from my heart using descriptive words and those based on feelings as opposed to incidents. At first, it took a lot of courage because not many people are willing to allow you to see the real them with the fear that if they reveal who they really are on a deeper level, one might not receive them, accept them, or be able to handle them. So, it takes courage to tell the story of who you are.

It takes courage to be who you are because your being sometimes causes you to tell a story even if you decide not to do it with your words. Your actions tell a story of who you are. It's the whole heart part that I wanted to add to this chapter. Speak from the heart regardless of how it sounds. It was that which lifted me. Spiritually, it was a burden that was lifted when I spoke from the heart and just told who I was. And the more I told who I was without the story behind it, the more I got back to who I knew myself to be way back when.

I started thinking that this was an exercise designed, unbeknownst to me, to reconnect me with who I knew myself to be from my source. When I was very young, up until early adulthood, I started living behind a number of story lines, based on how I saw my life, at the time. But the more I pulled back the layers of telling who I really was, the more I began remembering. I remembered when I won an award at summer camp and how I wanted to be a leader, how I loved helping people, how I listened to different kids and friends from different walks of life. I understood some of their challenges. But more importantly, I remembered the courage they had in the telling of their experiences that I didn't experience and how great that was.

Most of us are very open to tell who we are with all our hearts to total strangers. I'm sure all of us have walked into a grocery store, sat at the doctor's office, the bus stop, or anywhere we wait with other people. Strangers are quick to tell you who they are with their whole heart because they feel they're not going to be judged. They realize you don't know them well. You don't really have a basis for comparison, and they can just share. Most of the time it's from the heart because they typically don't use all of that precious time telling a stranger the entire story. It's that smile on your face when you're listening to a stranger pour their heart out that really allows you to see yourself and say, "Wow, I think my life's not that bad," or "My life is that bad, and there's some things I need to look at." But it really takes courage to tell who you are with your whole heart.

The opposite of that would be telling who you are without your whole heart because of bringing up some feelings of shame, guilt, or unworthiness or for fear of being judged. There are a number of incidents I can remember where I really felt that if I chose to be in business or a serious relationship with anybody, male or female, it was important that we spent some time actually telling who we were. What are we? Who are we ? Who have we been? Who do we know ourselves to be, and where do we want to go with this knowingness? That took heart, but it felt good at the end of the day.

i.

Willing to Let Go of Who I Thought I Should Be to Be Who I am

It's amazing because I can remember all the way back to finishing undergrad and obtaining my degree, beginning my first job as a teacher, and receiving my paycheck. I thought *Wow, is that it?* Although I set out to be an educator to help change my community by helping to shape young minds, I remember deciding at that point to go back to graduate school to be who I thought I was at the time. I was to become more enlightened, to gain an additional degree, and of course to make more money. I thought I should go back and provide but also look good. I mean, here was a young man who came from the meager beginnings of a single female-headed household to being the second person to graduate from college in my immediate family, and I was going on to graduate school.

As the second person in my family to obtain a master's degree, and after a couple of years of teaching, I thought it was supposed to be different for me. I thought I was supposed to be exempt from certain things. I thought I had arrived. I was a black man living in American with a master's degree, and I was very proud of that. Although my income didn't reflect that, it did remind me that I had obtained some goals that were very difficult; yet, I had accomplished them. The challenge was that I thought I was supposed to feel a certain way and look a certain way. I did! But, it wasn't good.

After a short period of time, I decided to walk away and give myself a chance to do something else. I left teaching to go on to other avenues to obtain money because I just wanted to see if I could. I wanted to be an individual. It wasn't that teaching didn't allow me to be an individual, but I just didn't see myself in that light once I arrived there. I had to let go of that part in order to get back out there to see who I thought I was, and that took a while. I'm still doing this as part of my journey.

I decided to go into consulting, and although I made the income, again that wasn't the issue. Once I made the money, I started spending more. I had a great time, but I started spending more. Then, I became broke on another level, proportionally the same, because I had exceeded my standard of living and bought some things for myself. Even at that point, I still had to be willing to let go of who I thought I should be in order to be who I am, because that wasn't it either, and I'm still on that journey.

Then, the marriage and the children came. It was time to have a family. All of my peers were doing it, and I was doing it, too. I wanted a family. Along with that I was choosing to become a new person. And although having children, being in a marriage, and creating a family is a great thing, one could get lost. There are all sorts of the things that come with that – children, bills, joining forces with a spouse, in-laws, buying houses, cars, more children, jobs, and careers. I just wanted to be a leader.

I always had a strong desire, although it has been refined, to live my life on my terms. I wanted to choose a vehicle where I could earn a living, but I also wanted to create my life on a daily basis. If I wanted to serve, I wanted to choose the manner in which I would serve. If I wanted to spend time with the children or if I wanted to travel, I wanted to go boundlessly. I knew a long time ago that all structures were designed to be dismantled after a certain amount of time, so part of me always had this spirit of individuality and spontaneity.

I decided to try a lot of things, which I hadn't shared with people, but that helped me gain who I now am. Who I am is very simple. I'm just a Being who showed up to play full out, to contribute, and to do something phenomenal. I'm not sure what that is, but I know that's the case. My skills and experiences have allowed me to be a leader and use my leadership skills to lead people. My experiences have also allowed me to serve and I enjoy helping people.

Who I am is a free-spirited person who loves to create a lifestyle in which I'm contributing, and at the end of the day I can feel alive - whether I'm volunteering, traveling the world, spending time with the children, or working a business deal. I had to go through all of what I thought society said I should do, and that included going to college, working, getting married, creating a family, finding a nice job, buying a house, a car, a dog, and waiting to die. But instead, I had to take some bumps in the road, and there were some losses and gains which came with that.

I can embrace them now, but at the time it wasn't so easy. It didn't exempt me from challenges, but the journey was worth it. I had to be willing to let go all of that. I had to be willing to let go of the idea of who I thought I should be, and I didn't want to. But I thought I should in order to be who I am now. Who I am now is constantly evolving, but it sure feels good to be here without a lot of the things I had. Although I miss some things that I had, I don't have any regrets. I do feel a shift, from a spiritual standpoint, of getting closer and closer to who I know myself to really be.

ii.

The Core of Shame and Fear

About six months ago, I listened to a seminar by Dr. Brene Brown, a professor at the University of Houston. She was presenting on a topic in which she discussed how feelings contribute to our way of being, how we make use of our feelings, and how they serve or make things complicated for us. One of the things she mentioned was the idea of shame and guilt. She described shame as the fear of connection. She said the less you talk about it, the more you have it. I used her explanation of shame and fear and connected it to how it's also the birth place of joy, creativity, belonging, and love because they all come from the same place. They all come from within, according to Dr. Brene.

Obviously, they are emotions, but the connection is the reason why we're all here. In order for us to connect, or in order for a connection to happen, we have to allow ourselves to be seen. I described previously that it takes courage to tell the story of who you are with your whole heart, also from Dr. Brene Brown's lecture. Shame will prevent that courage. Guilt will prevent that. Fear will prevent that, and it will all cause a disconnection.

Connection gives all of us purpose and meaning in our lives. We all can agree that life can sometimes be messy, but we are to love it anyway for who we are and for why we showed up. Sometimes that can be difficult, but we all have a sense of love and belonging, and all of us don't believe that we're worthy of that love and sense of belonging. What I've found in my personal life and by listening to Dr. Brown is that people who feel worthy have a sense of courage in common. They are comfortable, and they are courageous enough to tell a story of who they are or who they were with their whole heart.

It's that courage to be imperfect that allows us to be seen, and that is the basis for connection. You have to be willing to let go of who you think you should be in order to be who you are. Earlier, I explained how I was willing to walk away from what I thought was expected of me. I had to let all of that go to be who I am. I figured I had nothing to lose and everything to gain because, push came to shove, if who I thought I was or who I thought I knew myself to be wasn't okay, I could always go back to that by playing it safe and falling under predictability. But to fully embrace the joy, creativity, sense of belonging, and love it starts with us being vulnerable. According to Dr. Brene, vulnerability is the core of shame and fear, and it also happens to be the birth place of joy, creativity, belonging, and love.

After 11 years of marriage I didn't feel any more connected than I did the very first year. I thought maybe it was because of me; that I may have had a blockage. I thought that maybe if I was out of the way, my spouse at the time could gain the courage and tell the story of who she knew herself to be with all of her heart. I also thought that in my absence she would be willing to let go of who she thought she should be in order to be who she is. I was on that journey and I knew what it felt like. I didn't want to be the cause of somebody's inability to do that.

My ex-spouse wasn't completely ready to embrace vulnerability, although she did make some strides. No matter how often I said it, she had to get it for herself. I often told her that that which makes you vulnerable makes you beautiful. She didn't believe that because she wasn't willing to go there. Her not being willing to share and her stoppage around that forced her, in my opinion, to remain controlling, fearful and predicting. If she couldn't control, or she couldn't predict the outcome of anything or any situation, she wouldn't be willing to move forward.

The same place shame and fear remained was the same place that the joy, creativity, and belonging derived from. Once we learn vulnerability, we learn a lot of different emotions that come from that same place. When we numb the emotions, we numb the joy, the gratitude, and the happiness which causes the creativity and the belonging.

Why do we numb emotions? I'm not totally

sure. I believe a number of incidents in our upbringing causes us to numb emotions because as children we're pretty much hardwired for struggle and challenges. Not from a traumatic standpoint, but because we're open to learn, we take on struggle unless it's conveyed to us typically by the people around us (the adults) that life should be hard. A struggle is not insurmountable for us as children. We naturally take on the challenges of life. We naturally continue to learn or continue to practice while falling on our backside until we get it. We don't get that any another way. There's a naturalness that comes when we show up.

I practice gratitude and joy. I talked about being vulnerable and telling a story of who I am because at one time I had a lot of guilt and shame. It must have been buried because I wasn't aware of anything I held onto because I've always had someone close to me to share things with just as fast as it came. If there was something I was embarrassed or ashamed about, or afraid of I had a brother or a best friend to share it with. I have an older sister, and I've always had a ton of friends who I could also share with. So I didn't have to keep it inside where it could fester into some deeply rooted feelings, and where in order for me to sustain any type of workable relationship I would have to numb those emotions. So I thought! I later realized that numbing one emotion almost numbs all of them. There's a struggle to experience joy once you've numbed a number of other emotions because of guilt, fear, shame, and unworthiness.

Shame unravels our relationships and our connections with other people. Shame breeds fear, and it causes blame and disconnection. The core of shame and fear is also the birth place of joy, creativity, a sense of belonging, and love. I wish I had known that sooner.

iii.

Reasons I Use to Stay This Way

Throughout the majority of my life, most of my ways of being served me well. Most of them were derived either out of a sense of success or fear of failure. And what I learned was the reason I used them continuously is that they worked, or, at least they appeared to work short term.

I also learned a while ago that there's a difference between a cost and a pay-off. With most of the things we do in life towards ourselves and other people, we have a cost for them. They cost us dearly in some form or fashion – financially, spiritually, mentally, and emotionally. We have hopes of being paid off in those same areas.

I can remember coming up as the youngest of three and going to a different school than where my brother and sister were attending. When it was time for me to go, it seemed as if it was time for me to face the world on my own. I had to be tough. I was the last to leave the house. There was a sense of fear that I would have to go to school by myself, and it was at that moment that I chose to do things on my own. I developed a sense of toughness and courage to subside my fear. I remember actually saying to myself, "I'm all alone, and I have to do well to save myself." I used that as a reason for staying this way throughout my entire life. When it became time to make things happen, I just repeated that internal message to myself, and most of the time it worked out. My sense of fear coupled with my internal dialog was one of the reasons I used for staying this way, and as a result I developed some strong suits which allowed me to be successful.

The challenge came when I overused what I perceived to be strong areas, to a degree where they caused me to be too aggressive, too assertive, and unreasonable. And I always went back to the reasons I used for staying this way because I had conditioned myself to use them at a time when I knew they would make me very successful, and they did.

My fear-based strong suits were reasons I used for staying the same throughout business dealings and practices. Whenever I would sense fear within, it would actually pump me up to really tackle my fears head on. Since then, I've learned to do it more from a spiritual standpoint by just acknowledging my doctrine within, closing my eyes to meditate, and using breathing exercises. I don't have to use force any longer – I can use power from within because I now recognize my connection to the Most High. I still have to remind myself, from an awareness standpoint, that the reasons I used for staying this way don't always work, and I have to remain flexible on my journey.

- CHAPTER 5 -
I Decided to Be Childlike

Throughout the last few years, when I went into my protective state I decided to be childlike. I spent the majority of my time outside of my family, my children, and my business affairs to just be childlike. I hung out, I celebrated, and I did a lot of social activities to take my mind off my reality which was very painful at the time. However, I decided to focus on the things that made me laugh and stay in a childlike state. I realized that when things got tough (or when I perceived them to have been tough) or when I started overloading my mind with negative thoughts, I forced a smile on my face; and it literally changed my energy internally.

So whenever I have negative thoughts, I literally just smile. I still use that tactic, today. I stop and I become present for myself. I get centered and start my breathing exercises.

On the outside, I really focused on doing things that provided me social enjoyment and that also allowed me to go back to the essence from whence I came. I remember having a great childhood, lots of fun, organized sports, games with my siblings, tons of friends, sleepovers, and all types of things. I chose to go back to being childlike in feeling.

Coming from my mind and from the guidance of my mom as my spiritual leader I remember being fearless, being imaginative, and being happy all the time – I never experienced illness, never stayed overnight at a hospital, and had great times. I continue to remind myself now to be childlike and to focus on things that make me smile and laugh. I watch a lot of funny movies when things get tough – as a matter of fact, I decided to be proactive and fill up on funny things. I especially like meeting with a group of friends or family members and reminiscing on things or even making current things appear to be funny. It just kind of takes the sting off of life. I decide to be childlike and focus on the things that made me laugh which take me back to the essence of who I am as a child of innocence and also remembering when life was sweet —it's still sweet, and it's still great. It's when I get to go back and think of great times, reminding myself of an awesome childhood, that I am I able to continue on this journey. So, I tiptoe on my current journey in a childlike manner, and I spend at least some portion of my day laughing because it heals my soul.

We must all go back to being innocent little children, go back to the time when, in our minds, we didn't give a damn about what we thought seriously; we just did. We always operated in natural goodness. It wasn't until we grew old and started experiencing life that we forgot that inner guide that we were all born with.

In Ernest Holmes's *The Science of the Mind: A Philosophy, A Faith, A Way of Life*, he states, "We must return the way we came, as little children who know that life is good and to be trusted. We are to approach our problems as though they were not. Approaching them in this manner, they will vanish."

i.

Lean Into the Discomfort

As children, we show up already hardwired to

deal with discomfort. We take it on as children unless we're taught to fear and to obsess about that fear from adults around us. But, being uncomfortable as a child is something we take on. We lean into it. And to remain successful as an adult, I learned to go back to being childlike and lean into the discomfort that presented itself to me.

One of the ways I learned to lean into the discomfort is by beginning with the end in mind. Whatever came about that I perceived to be uncomfortable, I'd always start with the end in mind and predict the worst thing that could happen – financially, spiritually, and emotionally. I'd ask myself *What's the worst thing that could happen?*, and I'd start from that place and work myself backwards reminding myself that being uncomfortable is not as bad as it seems once I take my mind to the worst possible outcome. It never really turns out that way, but it eliminates the fear as I go through tackling the challenge once I start with the end and work my way backwards all in my mind.

As children, we did that. We leaned into the discomfort when we learned to walk, talk, eat, tie our shoes, tell time, and write and memorize our timetables. All those things, we leaned into and took it on as a challenge. So I encourage, not only myself, but other adults whom I work with to start briefly with using their mind to anticipate the worst possible outcome, knowing that it will not happen most of the time, and practice leaning into the discomfort.

ii.

A Way for Me to Discharge My Pain and Discomfort

Blaming someone else was a big one for me. This was one that not only myself, but most people I know, use to stray away, and actually hide from confronting themselves, or at least numb the pain. The biggest area I did this was in my previous marriage. I used the disconnection between myself and my ex-wife to keep me from focusing on the things I said I wanted to do, so I spent a lot of wasted time blaming her.

For me, not being able to move forward on things that I had planned for myself was difficult. I spent a lot of time blaming the marriage, how it was unfulfilling, and how it really drained me. And although there may have been some validity and truth to the pain, the blaming part is what kept me weak. It's what disempowered me. The more I continued to blame, the more I allowed my pain to become more powerful than I was. I later chose for myself and embraced the discomfort, uncomfortably.

Whenever it came about that I was uncomfortable, I would use that opportunity to stop and ask myself *what am I feeling now?* It was those few moments throughout the day that I used to talk calmly to myself while taking deep breaths which allowed that feeling of being uncomfortable to subside. Then it became my own little mental and emotional game that whenever I felt uncomfortable, I would just go into an immediate self-taught breathing exercise. It always worked.

For a long time, instead of dealing with my pain, I let it remain outside of my body. I took no responsibility while I was blaming and complaining. The more I blamed, the less I took personal responsibility. From a spiritual and deeper conscious level, I finally arrived at the place where I started asking myself *why is this happening for me?*, instead of blaming.

Again, I created another mental and emotional game, so whenever I blamed my ex-spouse about the failed marriage (or what I thought was a failed marriage), I would ask myself *Why is this happening for me? What is it that I need to get for myself to move to the next level?* And, more importantly, *how can I use overcoming this pain and discomfort and trying to shadow it with blame to help serve people who are either in a situation or something similar in terms of experiencing a loss?*

Blaming also creates what I consider to be one of those numbing emotions that, if you're not careful, can cause you to feel shameful and guilty. I knew that blaming was a fine line between feeling unworthy and feeling a sense of guilt. So when I peeled back the layers with questions like "Why am I blaming? Why am I blaming myself or anybody else who has caused me pain," I chose to remind myself that everyone, including myself, operates at their current level of consciousness. Although they may have or haven't caused pain to me, it's still more of a result of where they are consciously and spiritually more so than they actually did. Honestly, nobody caused me anything.

I also realized I didn't have that much power to control, predict, manipulate, or blame as much as I may have initially thought, in terms of who was responsible for what. I realized that all of us have a choice in our matter, and though I made a ton of mistakes, I would first master how my pain was not more powerful than me and then set out to teach people in how I overcame that pain. One of the first steps was to remove the blame game; and as we know, there's always a game to be played. Some of them are just more or less empowering than others.

iii.

Stop Controlling and Predicting

Controlling and predicting produces a smokescreen for fear. Whenever I chose to control or predict I was using force instead of power. The controlling part was my way of focusing more on what would happen if I didn't receive, accomplish, or achieve more so than what would happen if I did. And as we all know, what you focus on and argue for is what you continue to attract to yourself.

Whenever I went into this controlling and predicting state – and they always went hand-in hand –that was my way of using force as opposed to power. That was my way of using what I thought were tools outside of me, which actually drained me to the core at the end of the day, as opposed to using source; the strength and the universe of intelligence that was within me.

Predicting became my way of utilizing my

past and allowing my past to do the choosing for me. In other words, it was an old thought, not a fresh thought, which really performed mechanically. Whenever I saw, heard, or envisioned something that reminded me of my past, then my past would do the choosing or the predicting. This did not allow me an opportunity to create fresh thoughts or first thoughts to move into my consciousness where the universe could assist me and bring in the things I focused on to me. The controlling was fear-based. There's no need to control. There's no need to be controlled. I realized that all structures must be dismantled at some point. Trying to control a situation, or particularly an outcome, was my way of empowering the fact that on a deeper level the only reason I would seek to control was because I was afraid of not having, not doing, and not getting.

When controlling or predicting energies welled up within me, I used it as an opportunity to focus on meditating which allowed those feelings to subside. This was another opportunity for me to be present with myself, in regards to how I was feeling and thinking, and allow myself to be in the midst of those feelings without fixing or judging them – just allowing them to eventually pass. This took some practice – I'm talking months and years – and there were many times when I forgot to do that.

I equate everything to shooting a jump shot with a high field goal percentage or working out at the gym. It's those practice opportunities which are the same way we practice the things that don't work for us, and we focus and repeat over and over again. So, there's a lot of unlearning that we must do in different areas. And one of the biggest areas for most people I know, including me, is to stop controlling; stop strong-arming life and the things within it, but more importantly stop controlling people.

One of the greatest opportunities I have with my children is to create what's possible, to converse with them on a level where there's no control and they do not have to do things in a certain way at a certain time based on my control. They are led, they have input, they have say-so, and they have opportunities to practice it all.

It became this 'practice what we preach' thing, and the easiest way I used to demonstrate while I was practicing for myself was to make sure I was teaching that to my children. We teach the very lessons that we actually need to learn – it's not being a hypocrite it's just, in my opinion, a higher source giving us an opportunity to practice the lessons and ways we need to adjust. The awareness for me was in my way of examining it and really taking advantage of opportunities to forgive myself for controlling and predicting, forgive others for causing me pain and discomfort, and to actually live life on a deeper, richer level without all the force.

Forcing wears you out mentally, emotionally, physically. The power is within, and when we declare with conviction, with emphasis, and with the feeling of expectancy, the Universe immediately co-creates to bring us the very thing we are focusing on.

I eventually realized that controlling and predicting was a form of fear. At one point, it became neurotic for me. Sigmund Freud defined neurosis as a separation from self, and I knew that my real self was love and that I was separated. However, controlling and predicting was me expressing myself through fear and lack of Self-Love at the time.

I took a prayer from Marianne Williamson's, *A Return to Love,* book. In the section entitled "God," she explained how when she got into a terrible mess, not necessarily controlling and predicting, she'd remember to ask for a miracle, which caused her to have a shift in perception.

And she would pray, "God, please help me. Heal my mind, wherever my thoughts have strayed from love. If I've been controlling, manipulative, greedy, and ambitious for myself, whatever it is, I'm willing to see this differently." In her book, Marianne went on to explain how not only did she use this prayer whenever she found herself in a jam, but also before there was a jam. She just went into that space. I also use that prayer. I actually use it a couple times a week. I use it prior to finding myself in a mess.

I wrote that prayer down in my journal. I quoted it and used it on a semi-regular basis to assist me with moving past my addiction and my neurotic behavior of controlling and predicting. Just as Marianne described, it soon started dissipating. Even when it shows up now, I can stop – I do stop - and just become present to my force by going to the prayer or something similar.

- Chapter 6 -
More to Me Than I Have Given a Chance To

Recently, I've just decided to focus on all of the areas in my life that actually work for me. And what I realized is that there's more to me as a person, as an individual, and as a Being of God than I've really given a chance to. So I started to take a few moments every day to go back and remind myself of my success stories.

I went back as far as I could remember from childhood to where I am now and reminded myself of when I was acknowledged outside of myself for success. I remembered receiving an award for honor camper when I was younger and how I inspired all my fellow campers to really make sure that our cabin was number one. I had to be between eight and ten years old. I don't remember all the details, but I do know that there had to have been five to ten campers in the summer camp cabin. We won some type of award, and I was given a leadership award because they considered me to be responsible for getting us to do whatever it is we were recognized for. It was at that point that I said, "You know what? Maybe I am a leader. Maybe I do have the natural ability to inspire people – to really touch, move, and inspire people." So, when I look back at the common thread, there is more to me than I've given a chance to.

Since I was a child, I've inspired a number of people. And since I've become an adult, I've inspired children. I've inspired adults. In education, I've inspired colleagues and my students. As a consultant and an administrator, I've inspired teachers and other administrators, as well as business partners who were responsible for contributing to education. As a business professional I've inspired clients and business associates. Even when I was asked to coach with my friends and family and other people, I inspired them. I've also inspired significant others whom I've had intimate connections with. But now, I've chosen not to give myself another chance. I wasn't giving myself a chance to experience other areas of my life.

I have now chosen for myself that I would become a great leader, and I would be used by God to change the world as we currently know it; one soul at a time. I'm not sure in which area because, in the past, I've had success working with people regardless of the areas or objective. I've had success leading people. I've had success inspiring people. I've had success communicating with people. So I have decided to give myself more of a chance to step out on a larger scale to share with the world who I am, what I've experienced, and what I've learned through all of my experiences.

i.

Just Because I Can't See It Doesn't Mean It Isn't There

Initially I decided to approach this chapter from more of a faith-based standpoint. But then I chose to deal with it from a different angle. Recently, I decided to compile a list of questions that I would ask people who knew me well – friends, family, business associates, and people from different areas of my life, but who knew me very well. And based on their responses, I decided to extract the commonalities to see how I show up for other people. The majority of the people said I was stubborn but smart, courageous, a protector, a great friend, and other similar things. Although I wasn't shocked by any of the responses from people close to me, I did realize that just because I couldn't see things about myself, it doesn't mean that they did not show up. Asking a series of questions to people who knew me very well helped me to understand this. Some of the questions included what they thought about me, particular events, if they thought I lived by certain standards, and what were their earliest memories of me. I deeply understood that just because I can't see it –referring to that which I possess internally and externally – doesn't mean it isn't there.

ii.

Love and Uncertainty Exercise My Knowingness

A couple days after Christmas 2011, I received a call from my cousin. She called to ask if I would meet with her to talk. She said she just wanted to talk as cousins. I actually asked her what it was about, assuming it was something drama related, something that happened within the family that I wasn't aware of, or maybe something concerning my divorce or personal life.

Immediately, when she requested to speak with me, my mind went into a negative direction, and I started creating stories in my mind due to the uncertainty. But I loved her as my older cousin. We grew up together, talked before and I respected her. Because of the love, I decided to go out and meet with her.

I had to drop someone off in that area, so I used it as a win-win. The funny thing about this love and uncertainty I'm referring to is that, at the time, I was completely broke. I had absolutely no money and about a half tank of gas. As a matter of fact, I borrowed $2 from the friend I was dropping off just to buy my cousin a cup of coffee because we decided to meet for coffee. At this point in my life, I was so down-trodden and disgusted with life as I had borrowed money from most everybody I knew. I didn't even feel embarrassed to ask my friend for $2 to buy a cup of coffee for my cousin. So I took the $2, dropped the friend off, and immediately went to meet with my cousin. She actually picked up the tab for the two cups of coffee, which was great. She insisted on it. When she sat down, the first thing she said was, "I'm not sure how to say this, so I'm just gonna go ahead, you know, and just get right into it and say it." I was open and receptive, but my mindset was like, "Oh, what now?", because my strong suit of being tough had kicked in and because I was uncomfortable with dealing with the uncertainty. But I allowed the love of a family member to just move forward with it and I'm glad I did.

What was funny was that she sat down and – immediately after giving her intro about how this was difficult and how she's just going to come out and say it – she says something to the effect of asking me when I was in a very low place in my life, how did I come out of it. When she said that, I was overwhelmed and sad at the same time. I was happy that she thought enough to request my presence, to solicit my input, my feedback, and my counsel, but I was upset because I was actually still hurting. I was completely broke. I had no money, and I even struggled to get out to see her, but something within me told me to go ahead and do it.

The conversation we had was absolutely amazing! I let her know that I was honored and that this was great for me because I was in a terrible spot. And after listening and ministering to one another, we both walked away feeling much better and feeling more connected. We agreed to set up a meeting-place and a sharing time once a month, and it was life-changing.

Around the same time, another friend texted me and mentioned it was her birthday and asked would I stop by – she was meeting some friends. This happened right before I was supposed to meet my cousin, again - still in this funk, this brokenness, this wounded spirit, this financial challenge. I texted her and said, "Yeah." I agreed initially that I would come and meet her, and then I reneged through text saying, "Yeah, it's just not a good time," and that I'd make it up to her later. After talking to my cousin and being revived, I texted the friend back and told her I was going to come by and that I suddenly realized she didn't ask for anything. She just requested my presence. And again, with half a tank... less than half a tank... and the $2 that I'd borrowed from my friend to treat my cousin (who actually treated me); I stopped by to meet the friend. It was after meeting her that I felt even better because she just acknowledged my presence for her birthday. I stopped by for a few minutes as it was on my way home, and I felt amazing. Again.

That day ended with me feeling great. My cousin had solicited my input, and though I tried to pull out of going to my friend's birthday celebration, I went anyway as a result of speaking with my cousin. I felt revived. This exercised my knowingness that I had showed up to do great things; that people look to my presence; and that I was very grateful and humbled. In spite of my challenges and my financial situations, there was something in me. The love and uncertainty in these instances exercised my knowingness. I don't even know how, but it did.

I'm very grateful to my very close friend, who is now my beautiful wife, who loaned me the $2 to treat and meet with my cousin, who actually paid and who I shared with. We reconnected; she thanked me, and allowed me to meet another friend, in spite of being in the way of my own self. It was an awesome day, and the love and uncertainty in those instances continue to exercise my knowingness today. Even in your worst moments and while you're feeling awful, you must find a way to allow others to love you through it!

In his book *In Tune with the Infinite,* Ralph Waldo Trine – who is considered one of the greatest inspirational authors of all time – wrote,

> "We can be our own best friends or we can be our own worst enemies. In the degree we become friends with the highest and best

within us, we become friends to all. In the degree we become enemies to the highest and best within us do we become enemies to all. In the degree that we open ourselves to the higher powers and let them manifest through us, then, by the very inspirations we carry with us, do we become, in a sense, the saviors of our fellow men. And in this way, we all are, or may become, the saviors of one another. In this way, you may become indeed one of the world's redeemers."

iii.

I Couldn't Transcend While Continuing to Fight

Last night, I was up reading *In Tune with the Infinite* by Ralph Waldo Trine. In it, he says, "Discover for yourself the life-changing power." It's a classic – first published in 1897.

It was in the wee hours of the morning that I was fighting the frustration, the guilt, the pain, and the suffering - the self-induced suffering that I was holding onto because of the situation with my children and not being able to see them regularly. The night before, I was brutally honest with myself that I had resentment towards my dad, which allowed me to attract the very things I was trying to avoid with my own children. This further promoted my anger towards my ex-wife and kept me stuck. As I mentioned in previous chapters, this anger and resentment kept me stuck in a lot of different areas, primarily in being able to utilize my inner being as well as my efforts to make a living. I painfully realized that I couldn't transcend while I was continuing to fight within while blaming it on the disconnection with my dad and my ex-wife.

So one day, I woke up and called my dad. He had recently left me a couple messages and texts but I didn't respond. I called him for me, not because he'd left the messages. I called because I needed to make an emotional breakthrough for myself. And once I dialed the number, I felt really good about myself for having the courage to even call him.

I listened as he spoke. It lasted a couple minutes, and then we ended the call. I committed to myself that I would call him semi-regularly, primarily when I felt it. It seemed that when I ended the call, a weight - a burden – was lifted off my shoulders, and I felt good. It felt like a spiritual weight had just lifted – literally lifted – and I chose for myself that I was going to get past whatever hurt feelings and whatever stories I'd created. I was going to create continuous breakthroughs for myself regarding the relationship with my father.

So, going back to reading *In Tune with the Infinite* by Ralph Waldo Trine. It was about 5:00 or 5:30 in the morning and I read a passage that stuck with me. I don't even remember what it was exactly, but I was prompted to call my ex-wife, and let her know that I wasn't going to fight anymore. I was tired of fighting. I wasn't going to fight, and I didn't specify that I didn't want to fight because my experience had sort of conditioned me to fight. But I knew I couldn't transcend as long as I was fighting; and I've realized that for quite some time now.

I called, and she picked up. We agreed to talk again, so all-in-all it was a good conversation. We both got some things out. We stayed focused – at least I did – and I told her my desires and my plans for the children, for the support, and for her. We went back to some old agreements that was previously said. I didn't point the finger, nor did I spend time rehashing old events that caused pain on both our parts.

It was releasing the fight within me toward

my dad and ex-spouse that allowed me to get back into a space where I literally felt myself transcending – as I am right now. (As I'm speaking/typing right now, I literally feel a weight being lifted off the top of my head and shoulders.) It was unbelievable. I ended both calls with the sense of joy and empowerment.

I felt that I was back – not back to my old self or even one I was creating, but on a whole new level. I chose for myself that I would not suffer; I would not continue to allow external or internal things to cause me suffering because it does not allow me to transcend. It was those two calls that changed it for me, and it was almost instantaneous.

- CHAPTER 7 -
My Answers to Life's Answers

i.

Incarceration

On December 16th, 2013, I went to jail for a close to 60 day stay. I was released from the Douglas County jail on February 10th, 2014, which of course meant I spent Christmas, New Years, Super Bowl Sunday and Martin Luther King Jr.'s Birthday Day in a jail, in a large dorm with about 50 plus other inmates around the clock, 24 hours a day.

Now, this nearly 60-day jail stay was probably one of the best things that ever happened to me for a number of reasons. First, I know I attracted it to myself. Second, I'm clear about the laws of attraction and how it works, and it was confirmed through this experience. Third, a level of guilt that I'd held in, and didn't realize it at the time, caused me to bring this towards me internally along with a few other things externally – this jail stay. It actually leveled the playing field, and I'll tell you why in a second.

The day I went to jail, I felt it. I was subconsciously prepared for it more than I realized for a number of different reasons – from my attire, to me taking a particular driving route, and a number of other things. I won't go into details on what transpired, but it did involve challenges from a divorce almost three years ago, court dates, missed court dates, back child support payments, anger, and resentment.

What I received from that nearly 60-day stay was freedom from guilt, confirmation about what I contemplated, who I had become, and the opportunity to connect, help, serve, and be with other gentlemen who I would have otherwise thought were worlds different from me. In fact, we all had a lot in common.

I overlooked the guilt I had. I was upset about tons of other things, and I forgot that I had done a lot of terrible things out of spite. It wasn't settled within me. I think going to jail was my way of getting over the guilt and leveling the playing field in my mind, as well as getting some much needed rest and alone time.

I'm happy about being true to myself and becoming complete. I'm also happy about the people I met, the experiences, insights, and things I learned from my jail stay. There were a lot of misconceptions that I was able to put to rest about myself and other people.

One of the groups I'd like to serve as a mentor, speaker, teacher, lecturer, and guide is men who are incarcerated or who have been incarcerated. Having a first-hand experience of being incarcerated for close to two months brings tons of new and old things into perspective. I AM grateful for the brief opportunity to experience what so many Black Men have experienced. I don't ever plan on going back, but I get some things that no education, no book, no classroom, no podcast would have ever been able to expose me to.

Going to jail for nearly 60 days at the age of 42, spending the holidays completely locked down – and I mean, sleeping in the bunks, eating terrible food, showering every other day, and wearing a jumpsuit was probably one of my greatest experiences. I found who I was, I found who I needed to be, I found the group I needed to target, I found personal development and spiritual development, and I received a lot of intimate insights and details about myself and other people that I don't think I would have gotten any other place.

I actually willed my 60-day incarceration to myself through the laws of attraction and contemplation. I wrote my dissertation for my PhD in counseling focusing on Black Men and a program that I designed which focused on using spiritual laws to navigate anger, discouragement, and resentment among Black Men. I did a lot of research and read books about mass incarceration. During my research and shortly before my jail stay, I angrily read Michelle Alexander's book, The New Jim Crow. My dissertation topic came as a result of me taking a plea for something that was unresolved within. I embodied the entire mass incarceration circumstances, so living it within ultimately caused me to live it without; and I'm okay with that.

So today, I stand before you acknowledging all myself, truly acknowledging others, acknowledging my wife, and acknowledging my ex-wife. I am proud of myself for my commitment to myself. I am proud of myself for putting my head down, serving my time inside and out, and doing what I needed to do. I'm also proud of myself for allowing myself to meet myself on a different level. I'm proud of myself for being true to who I am.

I forgive myself for the guilt. I forgive myself for the fighting. I forgive myself for the abandonment. I forgive myself for the drama. I forgive myself for all of the causes within the last few years. I commit to myself to be the strong man that I am. I commit to myself to be a pillar in the community. I commit myself to others, to serving, to leading, and to guiding. I commit myself to my family. I commit myself to my children. I commit myself to my wife. I am who I know that I am, and who I am is courage, understanding, love, wealth, health, patience, peace, balance, wellness, and commitment. I AM Curtis Dominick Jasper and I thank you whole-heartedly for sharing this with me!

- 8 -
TRANSFORMATIONAL APPROACHES

From my personal experiences, these are what I've found to be the necessary healthy habits, attitudes and/or attributes that were needed by me, individually, as a pre-requisite for self-actualization. Amongst these, are: a wish to be oneself, to be fully human, to be completely fulfilled, to be completely alive, all while risking being vulnerable, and uncovering more 'painful' but critical aspects in order to learn about and grow through and integrate these parts of myself.

Self-actualization is a term I use to indicate the prominent feeling of being fully alive and aware of what it means to be a meaning-creating Human in an otherwise complicated universe. For me, it was the self-realization of my individuated maturity and growth in balance with my interdependent spirit. Self-actualizers have a healthy perception of reality, they know how to co-create their own realities (mind, body, and soul) by practicing healthy habits as a lifestyle.

#8

Here are Eight Transformational Approaches and my assigned meanings that I've used to overcome my obstacles.

1.) I started dialoguing with myself using a language beyond words

On my way to becoming self-actualized, I started becoming aware of the interconnectedness of all things. As such, I was able to form deep relationships with nature and energy. From these relationships I developed a profound nonverbal form of communication. It's in my body, resonating within my thoughts and muscle memory. I have to be still to hear it. I have to be silent to realize how loud it really is. By relearning this new, nonverbal language, I open myself up to the magnificence of the universe and allow for the innerworkings of nature to reattach itself through me. It became as simple as my body signaling me that I've consumed too little water or not enough rest, and as complex as the universe telling me what is the healthy way for me to live in an interconnected world with other people. Until I relearned this language, and once again engaged in a healthy dialogue with nature, myself and the universe, I continued to be misled by the less evolved aspect of myself and others. I AM now able to learn from this deep, rich dialogue with nature, self and the universe, and I AM rarely misguided by the less evolved aspects of myself, nature and other people.

2.) I begin to embrace solitude

I AM now able to get away from the cultural and mass-consciousness, matrix, rat-race and embrace and enjoy solitude on a regular basis. At any time, to lose one's Soul(ness) in our culture has become easily attainable. Most of us live in a matrix society of nine-to-five wage slavery, brainwashed into working jobs we don't like in order to buy things we don't need, but believing it to be the only way. Self-actualizers are aware of this. And even if we are currently stuck in such a pattern, we at least understand how important solitude is for us to breathe. In solitude with nature is where we can hear and learn a language beyond words. But losing ourselves in the wild is about rediscovering a balance between nature, the universe, energy and the human soul. It's about quieting the noisy ego with sacred silence. Solitude teaches us how to be quiet in order to reconnect. It also shares with us how to effectively and lovingly communicate with ourselves. I've found that the more I open up to the universe, the more the universe opens up to me.

3.) I became holistically creative

I was determined to connect the disconnected by using authentic creative expressions. I became extremely innovative and am now able to use rebellion as a tool for looking at things differently and not necessarily 'acting out'. I AM no longer driven by rage, revenge or egoistic competition. I now empathize and actualize as I disrupt with compassion and passion, seeking not to discredit and embarrass the status quo with my expressions, but to shock it into becoming more authentically awed with something new. I now celebrate the soul instead of the conditioning reactions of the ego. I celebrate through radical creative expression, and I love what I do. Weaving my knowledge and experience together in creative ways, I get to stir up the outdated, boring status quo while honoring my engagement with it.

4.) I begin practicing mindful meditation, daily.

When the creative power of the universe becomes conscious of itself, it manifests as joy. I get that you don't have to wait for something "meaningful" to come into your life so that you can finally enjoy what you do. As a Self-actualizer, I realize that the universe itself is vibrating at varying frequencies all in position to support each and every one of us. Essentially, mindful meditation is the act of familiarizing myself with my own unique contribution to the universe. Learning how to meditate is becoming present to the interconnectedness of all things. When I meditate I come to realize that I AM both the seer and the seen. I AM an extension of the universe becoming aware of itself. This is the importance of presence. Being in the moment, and especially being quiet and listening to what the moment has to say, is the foundation of healthy, mindful meditation.

5.) I started practicing Relationship-Based Love

As a Self-actualizer, I started practicing relationship-based love as opposed to the ownership-based love in any form. I AM now able to integrate rather than segregate. I understand that a healthy relationship is neither other nor self: it is both at once. We live in a world of immeasurably complex relationships that can only be understood when the veil of deceit and lies drops and we are able to engage with each other honestly, truthfully and respectfully. Self-actualizers are able to see through the smoke screens, inauthenticity and B.S., and can therefore engage each other with authentic in-the-moment presence. They can listen deeply, without having an agenda, and they understand that being truly loving is not achieving a state of invulnerability but achieving a state of absolute vulnerability. Compassionate honesty is my mantra and authentic communication is my only vehicle toward deep connection.

6.) I begin to let go and forgive

Two of the most difficult things most people can do in this world are to forgive and to let go. Self-actualizers are able to do both. I've learned to do both, after many years of practicing. I now have the ability to let others live the way they need to live and the ability to let things go. Letting things go is a painful process of maturity. It requires an almost perfect disposition toward reality. Perhaps the only other emotion more difficult to master is forgiveness. And sometimes we need both in order to grow and mature in life and in relationships. Self-actualizers understand this and are able to set their egos aside in order to love completely, holistically and with compassionate detachment. Letting go and acting with forgiveness is Large Mind Thinking, feeling, maturity and emotional intelligence.

7.) I became an emotional conversionist

Self-actualizers are conversionist. I learned the ability to transform my anger into strength, my fear into courage, and disappointment into compassion. I now know how to empower myself by controlling my "negative" emotions through "positive" action. As a Self-actualizer, I understand that the action is the thing. Inspired, positive action is really the thing. Most people act the way they feel. But this doesn't have to be the case. There is a choice. With enough discipline and practice we can all actually feel the way we act. You can "feel" scared but "act" courageous. With enough practice you can eventually feel the way you act. Through emotional conversion, happiness is a choice. Self-actualizers know how to transform aches and pains into pleasure points, wounds into wisdom, and weakness into strength. They make it a habit to consistently seize the moment and make the most of it.

8.) I learned a renewed appreciation for myself and my life, daily, like I did when I was a child.

As a Self-actualizer, I now know how to create a freshness of appreciation. After much practice, I now seem to constantly renew appreciation of life's basic goods. A sunset, date, newborn child, vacation, gift, pet, insect, dinner, workouts, walks, movies, or a flower will be experienced as intensely time after time as it was at first. I now possess a renewed "innocence of vision and feeling", like that of an artist or child. I do this on a regular independent of others, current happenings, present company or distractions, but primarily before I begin my day and before going to sleep. I show gratitude for life itself. I AM grateful for all happenings and I now take nothing for granted.

Open Letter to My Father

May 28, 2015

To My Father:

Happy Birth Anniversary to you, Sir! Today symbolizes your 71st turn around the SUN in the physical realm. I first want to apologize to you for who I thought I needed to be with you. Since your physical transition, I find myself struggling with the notion of not really knowing you. I knew of you, but I didn't allow myself to really get to know you. Receiving your fathership, love, and guidance was a foreign concept with me because I always felt you never invested enough time with me. Being raised primarily by a mother did not prepare me with the skillset…especially after my concocted story of who I thought you were.

I formulated a story about you many, many years ago, and you absolutely had no chance of acting outside the script I wrote for you. When I became old enough and mature enough, I still found myself without the transferrable skills to embrace you like I had for mom. I obviously get the distinction, but because I rehearsed my way of being regarding you my entire life, NO learning took place. We all know that learning takes place as a result of a significant relationship....I didn't realize your significance. I AM sorry for allowing myself to live out my concocted story and never really allowing you to get close. I knew your struggles coming up, and secretly, I always admired your strength, your charisma, your focus, and your tons of manners and ideas. I hated the fact that I lied to myself with a strong convince that you weren't there and that if you had been there (in the manner I thought sufficed) things for me would have been a lot different...a lot easier.

Back in December 2013, after I returned to Chicago to share in your memorial services, I heard a loud voice within me which told me to stay at your house. During the week at your place, I went through all of your things. As I looked through all of your photos and photo albums, I realized something absolutely embarrassing and painful! I realized that you were there for me...for us! You didn't make all the engagements, but you made the ones which really counted and more. You made the graduations! You made the little league games! You made the school assemblies! You made the birthday gatherings! You made the birth of the grandchildren! You made most! But because you weren't there on a daily, I discounted your existence…of course unless I needed something from you. My outdated, mastered story about your BEingness in my life disallowed me to remember those times. I apologize to myself and to you, dad! I forgive myself, and I forgive you, dad!

Since the years of your physical transition, I learned tons of things about myself. I wish I could say that I AM just like you, but that's simply not true. I AM not half the man you were! I AM not half the father you were! I AM not half the champion you were! I AM not half the giver you were! I AM getting there, and I thank you for allowing this to happen for me. You see, dad, with your physical representation still available, I would have continued to use you for my pain. I would have continued to blame you for my blindspots, shortcomings, child-rearing, marital challenges, and much, much more. I get YOU! I really do! I AM also starting to get me.

I LOVE how you continued to show up in

my life up until you passed on in December 2013. We hadn't spoken for more than 6 months, but you continued to call, leave messages, and text. I never replied. After mom's passing, I re-enacted my childhood story about you as I've always done. I came up with this crazy idea of trying to make you pay for Mom's physical death and the made-up of story of you not being there.

I've suffered a great deal. I AM much better, and I embrace it all. I thank the Creative Intelligence for allowing us to choose one another. I AM grateful for your existence, and I hope you will continue to guide me as you've always had.

Believe it or not, I took tons of information from your sharing, and some of my greatest achievements and successes were due to your guidance and your questions. What I really LOVED about you, Dad, is that you ALWAYS allowed me to be ME! You always allowed me to remain stubborn, arrogant, emotional, and sometimes down-right disrespectful. I AM sorry. Please forgive me. I see US…not you…not me, but US as I struggle with parenting, marriage, and other major areas in my life on occasion. I remember when you used to always say, "Just keep showing up!" I ALWAYS do!

Some of my greatest choices (painful ones)

were with your guidance. You always believed in me! It was you who encouraged me to stay at Murray Language Academy way back in 1979 when we moved back with mom in South Shore as opposed to transferring to the local neighborhood school. It was you who encouraged me to study Japanese for 9 years from 3rd grade until junior year in high school. It was you who hooked me up with a CTA bus driving summer position so that I could stack some money to return to college. It was you who encouraged me and dropped me off at Iowa State University even though I had already had plans to attend Clark. It was you who questioned me before my first marriage with a simple, but profound, question of which I've never forgot. I didn't get it then. I've paid dearly in a number of ways, but I get it! I get it! I get you! Rest in the Multiverses, Mr. Jasper. Please continue to look after me. I hope and pray that all of my children will one day get, accept, forgive, and embrace me completely!

With Gratitude,

Curt

ABOUT THE AUTHOR

Dr. Curt is a joyous Being, dad, friend and husband and the Founder of The I AM International, Inc. Foundation. Throughout the last 5 years, He's experienced multiple life changing events that he describes as "Necessary Integrative Inspirational Happenings." Among those life changing events were death, depression, homelessness, incarceration and a physical, mental and emotional disconnection from friends, family and children.

Through meditation, exercise, diet, spiritual work and the removal of toxic relationships paired with positive thoughts, words, actions, reactions and daily spiritual studies, Dr. Curt has been able to achieve health & wellness, weight loss, attain inner peace, create personal and professional success and demonstrate increased abundance in every area of life while remaining grateful and joyous during his journey. In his spare time, Dr. Curt enjoys weight training, hiking, reading, cooking, hanging with close friends, a plant-based nutrition and inspiring others to take positive steps in their own lives. Dr. Curt works, plays and sleeps right outside Atlanta, Georgia with his lovely wife, Angela.

You can find Dr. Curt on all social mediums and online at www.drcurtisdjasper.com

www.ingramcontent.com/pod-product-compliance
Lightning Source LLC
Chambersburg PA
CBHW060204050426
42446CB00013B/2990

9780692651179